50 Great Americans
Every Kid Should Know

Written by Jacqueline A. Ball
Illustrated by Tom LaPadula
Cover and sticker art
by Steve Haefele

If you have questions regarding this book or any of the
High Q™ workbooks, please call us, toll free, at
1-888-30 HIGHQ
(1-888-304-4447),
and one of our education specialists
will assist you.

Throughout our history, Americans have distinguished themselves in their lives and their careers. Fifty of these special people have been selected for this book. Their backgrounds and talents are very different, yet they all have something in common: Each has made a significant and lasting contribution to the world.

Browse through these fun-to-read biographies and colorful pictures and see history through the eyes of the people who helped shape it, including inventors, explorers, scientists, business leaders, civic leaders, social workers, athletes, judges, astronauts, champions of human rights—plus the many creative artists whose works and performances touched the nation's heart. These are people who believed deeply in themselves and their ideas, even if those ideas challenged the world in which they lived. Their vision—plus a lot of hard work—helped them accomplish their goals. As Thomas Edison once said: "Genius is one percent inspiration and ninety-nine percent perspiration."

This book is divided into six historical periods. Each one is introduced by a time line that highlights important events of the day, to help you see how our country grew over the years. Plus, there are fact boxes on every page that contain an especially interesting nugget of information about each person's life.

You will notice that the world of politics is not represented in this book; no U.S. Presidents have been included (although you will read about two First Ladies!). To learn about these great Americans, look for *The Presidents Sticker Book*.

Stickers

Pocahontas • Page 5

Benjamin Franklin • Page 6

Daniel Boone • Page 8

Patrick Henry • Page 9

Abigail Adams • Page 10

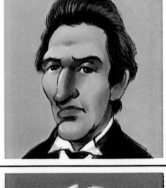

Phillis Wheatley • Page 11

Samuel Morse • Page 13

Horace Mann • Page 14

Frederick Douglass • Page 15

Walt Whitman • Page 16

Susan B. Anthony • Page 17

Clara Barton • Page 18

Harriet Tubman • Page 19

Andrew Carnegie • Page 21

50 GREAT Americans
Every Kid Should Know
Stickers

Mark Twain • Page 22

Alexander Graham Bell • Page 23

Thomas Edison • Page 24

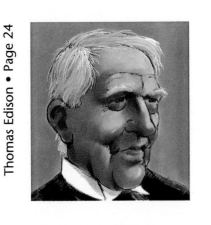

Samuel Gompers • Page 26

George Eastman • Page 27

Jane Addams • Page 28

George W. Carver • Page 29

The Wright Brothers • Page 31

Helen Keller • Page 32

Eleanor Roosevelt • Page 33

Georgia O'Keeffe • Page 34

CONTENTS

Meet these fifty great Americans
and learn about what they did!

1595 Pocahontas, daughter of Powhatan, born near what would soon be called Jamestown, Virginia.

1607 Jamestown founded—the first English colony to survive in America.

1612 Settlers plant tobacco in Virginia for the first time.

1620 The *Mayflower* lands at Plymouth, Massachusetts, carrying 102 Pilgrims in search of religious freedom.

1633 The first school in the colonies founded in New Amsterdam (now New York).

1692 Witchcraft trials held in Salem, Massachusetts.

1706 Benjamin Franklin born in Boston; a great inventor and civic leader, he establishes in Philadelphia the country's first public library.

1734 Daniel Boone born in Pennsylvania; helps open the West by blazing the Wilderness Trail into Kentucky.

1736 Patrick Henry born in Virginia; rallies colonies to fight for independence by proclaiming, "Give me liberty or give me death!"

1744 Abigail (Smith) Adams born in Massachusetts; becomes the country's second First Lady.

1749 Benjamin Franklin invents the lightning rod.

1761 Phillis Wheatley arrives in America as a slave; becomes a renowned poet.

1765 British Parliament passes the Stamp Act, levying taxes on the colonies' newspapers and other items printed on paper.

1773 Boston Tea Party—colonists board British East India Company ships that are carrying a cargo of tea and dump it in Boston Harbor.

1775 American Revolution begins.

1776 Declaration of Independence is signed on July 4.

Pocahontas
Born 1595 near Jamestown, Virginia
Died March 1617 in England
Family Married John Rolfe; one child
Claim to Fame Native American princess who helped early English settlers

broke out, and many people were injured or killed.

Then John Smith, one of Jamestown's leaders, was captured. His head was laid upon a stone, and he expected to be killed. But Pocahontas pleaded for his life. After that, John Smith became her adopted brother. Pocahontas began to help the settlers. She brought them corn

Pocahontas (which means "playful one") isn't just a character from a movie. She was a living, breathing woman—a real Native American princess who helped bring together the Old World of England and the New World of America.

Pocahontas was about ten years old when men from England arrived on three boats and settled near her tribe. They named their colony Jamestown, after the British King James. From the start, there were

bad feelings. Many Native Americans, including Pocahontas's father, the chief Powhatan, didn't trust the white settlers. Fighting

to eat and, when they got sick, taught them where healing plants grew in the forest. Without her help, the settlers of Jamestown Colony might not have survived.

It's a Fact
Pocahontas never had a romance with John Smith. She did marry another John—John Rolfe. Together they traveled to England. Everyone there wanted to meet the Native American princess—now known as Lady Rebecca Rolfe.

★☆☆★ BENJAMIN FRANKLIN ★☆☆★

Benjamin Franklin

Born January 17, 1706, in Boston, Massachusetts

Died April 17, 1790, in Philadelphia, Pennsylvania

Family Married Deborah Read; three children

Claim to Fame Colonial statesman who was also a printer, inventor, scientist, writer, and community leader

There he opened a print shop and started a newspaper, *The Pennsylvania Gazette.* He also published *Poor Richard's Almanack.* This reference book was published every year. It included a calendar, weather predictions, jokes, and poems. A character called "Poor Richard" narrated the almanac, expressing Ben's wise and funny advice. Sayings such as "A penny saved is a penny earned"

Benjamin Franklin went to school only from the ages of eight to ten. With 17 children, the Franklin family couldn't afford to pay for more education. But Ben didn't let that stop him. He read every book he could get his hands on. He taught himself everything from Italian to geometry.

At the age of 12, Ben began to work in his brother's print shop. He did a good job, but he and his brother didn't always get along. So at 17, he headed off on his own to Philadelphia.

and "Fish and visitors stink after three days" are often still heard today.

BENJAMIN FRANKLIN

Ben's curious mind worked like lightning. His most famous experiment caught lightning itself! In 1752, he used a kite to pull an electric charge down from the clouds, showing that lightning is electricity. He also knocked himself unconscious once while trying to shock a turkey. Instead, he said, he shocked a goose—himself!

Franklin was early America's most successful inventor. He never filed a patent (a legal document claiming ownership) for his inventions or took a penny in profit. He felt everyone should benefit from progress.

Franklin helped to make Philadelphia the most modern city in the colonies. He set up the first city postal system, helped start the first public library, founded the University of Pennsylvania, and started the first city hospital. He even organized the first volunteer fire company.

Franklin stove

Franklin was a skilled diplomat (a spokesperson for his nation). He traveled to France and convinced its leaders to support the colonies in their fight against England. Many historians say that without Ben Franklin, America might well have lost the Revolutionary War.

Ben put his ideas to work in shaping the new nation. He helped write the Declaration of Independence and the U.S. Constitution. In the year he died, at age 84, he signed a petition asking Congress to end slavery. He was a great statesman who worked hard for fairness all his life.

It's a Fact
Ben Franklin invented the Franklin stove, the lightning rod, and bifocal (double-lens) eyeglasses.

Daniel Boone

Born November 2, 1734, near Reading, Pennsylvania

Died September 26, 1820, in St. Charles, Missouri

Family Married Rebecca Bryan; ten children

Claim to Fame Pioneer who helped open the West to settlers

In 1769, few settlers knew the way to Kentucky, a place where there were great numbers of buffalo, deer, and turkeys. But Daniel found a way there through the Cumberland Mountains and opened a path to the West for other settlers. This path became known as the Wilderness Road. Boone built a fort at the end of the Wilderness Road's northern fork, at a

place that was later called Boonesborough. Boone settled there with his family.

As white people moved in, they often fought with the Native Americans in the area. In 1778, Daniel was captured by Native Americans, but he escaped five months later.

Daniel Boone later moved to West Virginia and then to Missouri. By finding paths through the wilderness, he helped push the frontier—the border beyond which settlers had not explored—farther and farther west. He was one of America's greatest pioneers.

As a boy, Daniel Boone liked nothing better than to explore the woods. His father gave him a rifle when he was 12, and he loved to hunt. When his family moved to the wilderness of

North Carolina, Daniel helped his father work their farm. But he prayed for rain so he could go hunting. In the woods he became friendly with Native Americans who taught him many wilderness skills.

It's a Fact

Daniel Boone is often shown wearing a coonskin cap, but he actually wore a black felt hat.

Wilderness Road

PATRICK HENRY

Patrick Henry
Born May 29, 1736, in Hanover County, Virginia
Died June 6, 1799, in Red Hill, Virginia
Family Married Sarah Shelton; six children. Married Dorothea Dandridge; eleven children
Claim to Fame Patriot and statesman known for his wonderful speaking ability

On March 23, 1775, Patrick Henry delivered his most famous lines: "Give me liberty, or give me death!" He convinced many people that the colonies would have to fight for independence from England. Henry served as governor of the commonwealth (later the state) of Virginia for five terms.

In 1799, at age 63, tired and ill, Patrick made one last public

Even as a young boy, Patrick Henry spoke and argued so well that he could change people's opinions. As he grew older, he got even better at these skills. For a while, Patrick ran his own general store, where political arguments often rang out among the vegetables and bolts of cloth.

It was not surprising, therefore, that Patrick became interested in the law. After his store failed, he decided to go to court to watch lawyers argue their cases. Before long, he was studying his own law books, and soon he became a lawyer. In 1764, he was elected to the Virginia House of Burgesses, which governed the colony.

When England passed the Stamp Act, taxing the colonies, Patrick spoke out against it. He became a member of the Continental Congress, a group of men who met to discuss the future of the colonies, and advised that Virginia arm itself against England.

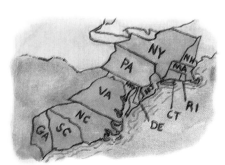

The Thirteen Colonies

speech. During a campaign for the Virginia State Legislature, he spoke to Virginians about how important it was to think of themselves as part of the new nation. The crowd was silent as he reminded them, "United we stand, divided we fall."

It's a Fact
Patrick Henry was invited to take all these jobs: U.S. Senator, Secretary of State, Chief Justice of the Supreme Court, Minister to Spain, and Minister to France. He refused all of them.

★ ☆ ★ ABIGAIL ADAMS ★ ☆ ★

Abigail Smith Adams
Born November 11, 1744, in Weymouth, Massachusetts
Died October 28, 1818, in Braintree (now Quincy), Massachusetts
Family Married John Adams; four surviving children
Claim to Fame The nation's second First Lady, whose letters give a detailed picture of early American life

When Abigail Smith was growing up, most girls didn't go to school. But she loved to learn and taught herself to read and write.

At 19, Abigail married John Adams, a young lawyer. In 1774, John was asked to represent Massachusetts at a meeting, or Congress, of all the colonies in Philadelphia. He remained there for most of the next two years. They wrote long letters to one another, discussing the fight for independence as well as family matters. Abigail Adams suggested that the Declaration of Independence should include rights for women: "the Ladies... will not hold ourselves bound by any Laws in which we have no voice." It was well over 100 years before the battle for votes for women was won.

From the Adams farm in Braintree, Abigail watched and wrote about some of the battles of the Revolutionary War. Between 1778 and 1788, John represented the government of the newly formed United States in France, Holland, and England. He and Abigail continued their correspondence until she was able to join him in 1784. In 1789, on their return home, John was elected

the first Vice-President of the United States, under President George Washington.

In 1796, Abigail became the second First Lady of the United States when John was elected President. She was the first First Lady to live in the presidential mansion (now called the White House) in Washington, D.C.

Abigail held several jobs during her lifetime—mother, farmer, writer, hostess. Because of the time in which she lived, she earned no money or official recognition for all her work. However, her journal and her many letters give us a vivid record of a strong, smart, and active woman.

It's a Fact
Abigail Adams was not only the wife of the second President of the United States, but also the mother of the sixth President, John Quincy Adams.

Phillis Wheatley
Born Probably 1753, in Senegambia, Africa
Died December 5, 1784, in Boston, Massachusetts
Family Married John Peters; three children who died in infancy
Claim to Fame Slave who became a famous poet

she was the author, the poems were published. As people learned about her brilliance, they gave her books, which were real luxuries at the time.

Phillis traveled to England, where people admired her work. She returned to Boston when she learned that Mrs. Wheatley was dying. Freed after the death of the Wheatleys, Phillis married John Peters.

One day in 1761, a little African girl stumbled off a ship, the *Phillis*, and began a new life as a slave in America. She was just seven or eight years old. She was bought by Susannah Wheatley, wife of a rich Bostonian tailor. Susannah and her husband John named the little girl after the ship which had brought her to Boston, and gave her their own last name.

Susannah Wheatley thought so much of Phillis's poems that she wanted to have them published. Some people did not believe that a slave could write poetry. But when Phillis proved

Phillis Wheatley was the first widely-known African-American poet. She wrote poems on many subjects, including war and African Americans. Her work, considered serious and elegant, was a great gift to the world.

The Wheatleys were very kind to Phillis. They taught her to speak, read, and write English. She learned Latin and studied the Bible. At age 12, she wrote her first poem. The Wheatleys were very impressed with her talent and invited some famous people in Boston to hear Phillis's poems.

It's a Fact
Phillis Wheatley wrote a poem praising George Washington. He liked it so much that he invited her to visit him. They met in 1776.

1787 ⭐ First official U.S. coin minted. In the design are the words "We Are One."

1787 ⭐ The U.S. Constitution signed on September 17.

1789 ⭐ George Washington elected President.

1791 ⭐ Samuel F. B. Morse born in Massachusetts; in 1844, invents the telegraph.

1791 ⭐ Bill of Rights adopted—ten amendments to the Constitution guaranteeing basic freedoms for all Americans.

1796 ⭐ Horace Mann born in Massachusetts; works to improve the public school system in America.

1803 ⭐ The Louisiana Purchase—U.S. buys 828,000 square miles of land from France, doubling the size of our country.

1806 ⭐ Meriwether Lewis and William Clark return to St. Louis after their expedition to the Louisiana Territory.

1812 ⭐ War of 1812 (between U.S. and Great Britain); British burn U.S. Capital and White House.

1814 ⭐ Francis Scott Key writes "The Star-Spangled Banner" following the battle of Fort McHenry.

1817-1818 ⭐ Frederick Douglass born into slavery in Maryland; later escapes to the North and becomes a great abolitionist.

1819 ⭐ Walt Whitman born in New York; writes beautiful poetry celebrating America and its people.

1820 ⭐ Susan B. Anthony born in Massachusetts; works to secure women's right to vote.

1821 ⭐ Clara Barton born in Massachusetts; founds the American Red Cross.

1821 ⭐ Harriet Tubman born in Maryland; helps hundreds of slaves traveling on the "Underground Railroad."

1825 ⭐ Erie Canal opens, creating a faster route between the Hudson River and the Great Lakes.

1829 ⭐ Andrew Jackson elected President—first "common man" in the White House.

SAMUEL MORSE

Samuel F. B. Morse
Born April 27, 1791, in Charlestown, Massachusetts
Died April 2, 1872, in New York, New York
Family Married Lucrece Walker; two children
Claim to Fame Artist who invented the telegraph and Morse Code

very little money, but he didn't give up because he believed so strongly in his idea. It took him many more years to get the invention accepted. Finally, on May 24, 1844, he tapped out the first telegraph message: "What hath God wrought?" It traveled from Washington, D.C., to Baltimore, Maryland, a distance of 35 miles.

The boy everyone called Finley grew up to be Samuel Morse, one of the most important inventors of his time. In school, he often got into trouble for drawing pictures instead of doing his work. He even drew cartoons of his teachers.

But Samuel had real talent. After studying science at Yale University, he went to study art in London. Although he painted portraits of famous people, he could not earn enough money to live on.

On a boat trip home from Europe, Morse joined a conversation about magnetism and electricity. When he learned

MORSE CODE

A .−	K −.−	U ..−	5 .....
B −...	L .−..	V ...−	6 −....
C −.−.	M −−	W .−−	7 −−...
D −..	N −.	X −..−	8 −−−..
E .	O −−−	Y −.−−	9 −−−−.
F ..−.	P .−−.	Z −−..	0 −−−−−
G −−.	Q −−.−	1 .−−−−	
H	R .−.	2 ..−−−	
I ..	S ...	3 ...−−	
J .−−−	T −	4 ....−	

that electricity travels instantly through any length of wire, he had an idea. He would create a machine that sent messages along a wire.

For the next five years, Samuel worked on his machine. He also developed a code of short and long taps to use with it. He had

The telegraph changed the world. With Morse's invention, people could send and receive messages instantly. Distances no longer seemed so great.

The telegraph changed Morse's life too. He became famous—and rich. He donated a lot of money to schools, churches, and poor artists.

It's a Fact
Morse was so poor while he was working on the telegraph that he couldn't afford to buy whole reels of wire. Instead, he found and bought short pieces of wire and joined them together with melted metal.

Early telegraph

Horace Mann
Born May 4, 1796, in Franklin, Massachusetts
Died August 2, 1859, in Yellow Springs, Ohio
Family Married Charlotte Messer. Married Mary Tyler; three children
Claim to Fame Lawyer who fought for free public schools for American children

Horace did extremely well at Brown. He became a lawyer and served in the Massachusetts legislature. When Massachusetts created a state board of education, Mann became its first leader.

Horace was deeply troubled by the public schools in Massachusetts. The buildings were dirty, the teachers were untrained and badly paid, and the school year lasted only a

Like most children at the time, Horace Mann went to school only nine or ten weeks each year. When he was 16, though, he spent six months studying with a private tutor. After this hard work, he entered Brown University in Rhode Island.

few months. Over the next 12 years, Horace worked to improve both the schools and the teachers. He started schools to train teachers, raised their salaries, bought school equipment, and increased the school year to six months.

Later, Horace was chosen to be the first president of Antioch College in Ohio. He stayed there for the rest of his life. Horace Mann's leadership in education helped improve public schools all over the country. Thanks to him, all Americans are entitled to a good, free public education.

It's a Fact
In his last speech Horace Mann said, "Be ashamed to die until you have won some victory for humanity." Horace Mann died unashamed.

FREDERICK DOUGLASS

Frederick Douglass
Born Probably 1817 or 1818, in Talbot County, Maryland
Died February 20, 1895, in Washington, D.C.
Family Married Anna Murray; five children. Married Helen Pitts
Claim to Fame Writer and former slave who educated the world about the evils of slavery

Frederick Douglass was born into slavery on a farm in Maryland. He lived the harsh life of a southern slave. He had few clothes and was fed little besides cornmeal mush. He often saw friends and relatives beaten and whipped. When he was eight, he was sent to live with new owners, Mr. and Mrs. Auld, in Baltimore. There, Mrs. Auld secretly taught him how to read. In turn, he began teaching other slaves to read.

When Frederick was 21, he made careful plans to escape to the North. He rode three trains and four boats to get to New York City. At last, he was free.

Frederick later settled in New Bedford, Massachusetts. There he met William Lloyd Garrison, a powerful abolitionist—someone who believed in ending slavery. Garrison hired Frederick to speak of his own experience as a slave. Frederick also wrote an autobiography describing his life as a slave. Because his book put him in danger of being captured and returned to his owners, Douglass sailed to England. There he spoke against slavery

and gathered many followers. Friends in England eventually bought Frederick's freedom from his owner.

When Douglass returned to the United States, he started an anti-slavery newspaper, *The North Star.* He became part of the Underground Railroad, a network of people and "safe houses" that helped African Americans escape to the North and to Canada. He also urged African Americans to fight for the North in the Civil War. After the war and the end of slavery, Frederick continued to speak out for the rights of African Americans and women. He was such a talented speaker that many people didn't believe he started life as a slave.

WANTED
F. DOUGLASS RUNAWAY SLAVE

It's a Fact
Douglass's original last name was Bailey. He changed it after he escaped to the North.

★ ☆ ★ ☆ WALT WHITMAN ☆ ★ ☆ ★

Walt Whitman
Born May 31, 1819, in West Hills, New York
Died March 26, 1892, in Camden, New Jersey
Family Second of nine children
Claim to Fame Poet who wrote one of America's best-known collections of poetry

Walt Whitman grew up on a quiet farm. When he was just 11, he quit school and went to work. Walt was a boy who didn't like to be told what to do. But he did like to talk, and he often rode on stagecoaches and ferries, just for the fun of talking with strangers.

Walt got a job in a newspaper printer's office at age 12. There he set lines of type, letter by letter, and began to see words as things that could be touched, moved, and molded. Later, Walt wrote stories and articles for magazines and newspapers.

He also wrote poetry. The poems in his great collection, *Leaves of Grass,* celebrate the cycle of birth, life, and death. They were written in a style no one had ever seen before: long lines of unrhymed verse. The poems celebrated the common man and woman, and the freedom and beauty of America. Walt could not find anyone willing to publish his work. He sold his house so that he could publish the first edition himself. *Leaves of Grass* quickly became popular in Europe. But many years passed before Americans began to admire it too.

Walt Whitman loved America. He showed those feelings through both his poems and his actions. During the Civil War, he volunteered in hospitals, binding wounds and reading to injured soldiers. He wrote a poem called "The Wound-Dresser" about this experience:

The hurt and wounded I pacify
*   with soothing hand,*
I sit by the restless all the dark
*   night, some are so young,*
Some suffer so much. . . .

Whitman continued to write articles and verses throughout his life. But he once said, "The United States themselves are essentially the greatest poem."

It's a Fact
Whitman published nine editions of *Leaves of Grass* during his lifetime. He felt that as he changed and matured, so should his work.

★SUSAN B. ANTHONY★

Susan B. Anthony
Born February 15, 1820, in Adams, Massachusetts
Died March 13, 1906, in Rochester, New York
Family One of five children
Claim to Fame Champion of equal rights who fought for the right of women to vote

Susan B. Anthony was born into a free country—free, that is, for white men, but not for slaves or women. Slaves belonged to their masters, and wives belonged to their husbands. Wives could not own property or keep any money they earned. Single women were no better off. Kept out of colleges and from most jobs, many had to work 12 hours a day in factories—for half the pay a man got. And no woman had the right to vote.

During this period before the Civil War, abolitionists (people who wanted to end slavery) often met at the Anthony home. Susan became active in their work. At the same time, she was growing more aware of how unequal women's rights

were—or, as she called them, women's wrongs.

By 1869, slavery had been outlawed, but women still did not have suffrage, the right to vote. Susan founded the National Woman Suffrage Association. She traveled all

over the country, gathering support for an amendment to the Constitution to give women the right to vote. In 1879, the "Susan B. Anthony Amendment" was presented to Congress—and defeated.

Susan died without seeing her lifelong goal come true. But she never lost hope that someday women would be equal under the law. In her last speech, she said, "Failure is impossible." She was right. On August 26, 1920, the 19th Amendment was passed, giving voting rights to women. The wording was exactly the same as the Susan B. Anthony Amendment of 1879.

It's a Fact
Susan B. Anthony became the first American woman whose portrait appeared on U.S. money—the silver dollar.

CLARA BARTON

Clara Barton
Born December 25, 1821, in North Oxford, Massachusetts
Died April 12, 1912, in Glen Echo, Maryland
Family Youngest of five children
Claim to Fame Brave nurse who organized the American Red Cross

As a young girl, Clara Barton was a shy child who lost her voice whenever she got very nervous. But even then she had a strong need to feel useful—to help people as much as she could.

When Clara was only 17, she overcame some of her shyness and became a teacher. Clara was a great success, and her shyness slowly faded. But after 15 years of teaching, she was ready for a new challenge.

In the 1850s, Barton moved to Washington, D.C. At that time there was much talk about the southern states leaving the northern states and starting their own country. In 1861, that's exactly what they did. Soon the Civil War began. Clara learned that there were few supplies for the North's wounded soldiers. She managed to locate bandages and medicine, and she nursed wounded soldiers all through the war.

After the war, while Clara was in Switzerland, she visited the International Red Cross. The work it was doing in Europe excited her. She decided that she would start a branch of the Red Cross when she returned to the United States.

With Clara as its leader, the American Red Cross helped victims of floods, forest fires, starvation, earthquakes, sickness, and war. Today, the Red Cross still helps people all over the world.

It's a Fact
Clara Barton worked as president of the American Red Cross until she was 82 years old!

Clara in her Red Cross uniform

HARRIET TUBMAN

Harriet Tubman
Born Probably 1821 in Dorchester County, Maryland
Died March 10, 1913, in Auburn, New York
Family Married John Tubman. Married Nelson Davis
Claim to Fame Ex-slave who helped hundreds of slaves reach freedom on the Underground Railroad

Harriet Tubman was born a slave on a plantation, a large farm. Even when she was young, she thought about escaping. When she was 28, the man who owned her died. All the slaves on the plantation were afraid they might be sold to other owners and never see their family and friends again. Harriet thought about running away, even though it was a crime, and the

punishment was harsh. Late one night, she left the plantation. She moved quickly and silently from Maryland to Delaware to Pennsylvania, where she became a free woman.

A year later, Harriet returned to Maryland to help other members of her family escape. Then she joined the Underground Railroad, a group of people who hid slaves in "safe houses" on their way to freedom.

Harriet in disguise

Often cleverly disguised, Harriet made many trips to Maryland and brought hundreds of slaves safely north to freedom. With each journey, she risked her life and her own freedom. When President Lincoln issued the Emancipation Proclamation, freeing slaves living in the Confederate states, Harriet's work was over. Until the Civil War—between the northern and southern states—ended, she worked as a nurse and as a spy for the North.

Harriet Tubman was extremely proud of the role she had played on the Underground Railroad. As she once said, "I never ran my train off the track and I never lost a passenger."

It's a Fact
Harriet Tubman was known as "Moses" because she led so many people to freedom, just as Moses had led the Israelites out of slavery in Egypt. At one point, there was a reward of $40,000 offered for her capture.

TIME LINE: 1835–1864

1835 Andrew Carnegie born in Scotland; a successful industrialist, he donates millions to establish universities and libraries in America.

1835 Mark Twain (Samuel Clemens) born in Missouri; creates the beloved book characters Tom Sawyer and Huckleberry Finn.

1839 Joseph Cinque leads a mutiny on the slave ship *Amistad*. Though later captured, Cinque and his companions win their struggle for human rights—they are declared free by the U.S. Supreme Court.

1844 Samuel Morse sends first telegraph message, which travels from Washington to Buffalo and reads: "What hath God wrought?"

1846 Territorial and border disputes between the U.S. and Mexico spur the Mexican War.

1847 Alexander Graham Bell born in Scotland; moves to America as a boy, and in 1876, invents the telephone.

1847 Thomas Alva Edison born in Ohio; in 1879, invents the electric lightbulb. Receives a total of 1,093 patents for his inventions!

1849 California Gold Rush begins.

1850 Samuel Gompers born in England; moves to America at age 13, and becomes a champion of workers' rights.

1852 Harriet Beecher Stowe publishes *Uncle Tom's Cabin*, a novel about the evils of slavery.

1854 George Eastman born in New York; an inventor, he introduces the Kodak camera in 1880.

1860 Jane Addams born in Illinois; dedicates herself to improving the lives of the poor in Chicago, and in 1931, becomes the first American woman to win the Nobel Peace Prize.

1861 Civil War begins between the Northern states and the Southern, or Confederate, states.

1863 The Emancipation Proclamation frees all slaves living in Confederate states.

1863 Lincoln's Gettysburg Address memorializes the men who died in battle.

1864 George Washington Carver born in Missouri; a talented agriculturist, he discovers new uses for peanuts and sweet potatoes.

Andrew Carnegie
Born November 25, 1835, in Dunfermline, Scotland
Died August 11, 1919, in Lenox, Massachusetts
Family Married Louise Whitfield; one child
Claim to Fame One of the richest men in the world, who used his wealth to help others

make steel from iron ore. At the same time, a huge amount of iron ore was discovered. These events helped the Carnegie Steel Company grow into one of the largest steel plants in America.

In 1901, Andrew sold his company for over $250 million. Then he began to use the money he had made to help

Andrew Carnegie grew up in Scotland, the son of a poor weaver. The family moved to the United States when Andrew was 12. They settled in Pittsburgh, Pennsylvania. Andrew went right to work in a factory.

Andrew's birthplace

Andrew was fascinated with Morse Code and telegraph work and became an expert at sending and receiving messages. When he was 17 and got a job

as a telegraph operator for the Pennsylvania Railroad, his life changed amazingly. Noticing that wooden railroad bridges fell apart very quickly, he helped start a company that made iron bridges. Then he helped develop a new way to

other people. He wrote books and articles about business. His money built over 2,500 public libraries and several colleges. Carnegie also believed that war was a great evil and gave rewards to people who worked toward peace in the world.

There are colleges, universities, corporations, awards, funds, and libraries named after Andrew Carnegie all over the United States. His generosity has helped millions to enjoy books, to study, and to learn.

It's a Fact
Andrew Carnegie gave away $288 million in the United States alone—to support education and peace.

Mark Twain (Samuel Langhorne Clemens)
Born November 30, 1835, in Florida, Missouri
Died April 21, 1910, in Redding, Connecticut
Family Married Olivia Langdon; four children
Claim to Fame Humorous writer and lecturer who created Tom Sawyer and Huckleberry Finn

Mark Twain was an excellent watcher and a great listener. He studied how people lived and talked. Then, in his books, he created funny characters who seemed as believable as people the reader knew. Twain once said that all his characters, even the villains, were based on people he knew. He once described a character this way: "Barring that natural expression of villainy which we all have, the man looked honest enough."

M ark Twain wasn't always a writer. He wasn't even always Mark Twain. Born Samuel Clemens, he grew up in Hannibal, Missouri, a town on the Mississippi River. One of his first jobs was piloting a riverboat. Boatmen used long poles to make sure the water was deep enough for the big riverboats. When the water was two fathoms (12 feet) deep and the boats could steam through, the men would call out, "Mark twain!" (Twain means "two.") Clemens liked the sound of "mark twain" so much that he took it for his pen name.

The piece that made Mark Twain famous was the humorous story "The Celebrated Jumping Frog of Calaveras County." In honor of that story, many towns around the country still hold frog-jumping contests every year.

Twain went on to write several novels. His best-known books are *The Adventures of Tom Sawyer* and its sequel, *The Adventures of Huckleberry Finn*. Generations of readers have enjoyed the humor and suspense of these stories. Tom Sawyer whitewashing the fence, and Huck and Jim on the raft in the river are two famous scenes.

It's a Fact
Mark Twain was born the year that Halley's Comet appeared. He predicted that he would die when the comet returned (75 years later). He was right!

Alexander Graham Bell
Born March 3, 1847, in Edinburgh, Scotland
Died August 2, 1922, in Nova Scotia, Canada
Family Married Mabel Hubbard
Claim to Fame Teacher of the deaf and inventor of the telephone

Alexander Graham Bell grew up in a family that was dedicated to helping deaf people speak. He started a school for the deaf in Boston, which later became Boston University. His wife, Mabel, was deaf, and Bell was always searching for ways to help her.

Early telephones

Bell was constantly experimenting with ways to make speech travel. In 1874 he figured out how to send voice sound waves over telegraph wires. Then he turned his discovery into an amazing new invention, the telephone. On March 10, 1876, Bell's assistant, James Watson, suddenly heard these words coming over the wire: "Mr. Watson, come here. I want you!" Bell had made the first phone call in history—from the next room.

The following year, Bell founded the company that carried his name and invention all over the world—the Bell Telephone Company. But he didn't hang up his imagination just yet. He created the photophone, which sent speech by light waves. He invented the audiometer, which measured people's hearing. And he made the first wax recording cylinder—which, combined with a disk, led to the phonograph.

Later in life, when he became interested in flying, Bell designed a kite big enough to carry a person through the air. He also improved the design of airplane landing gear. In one of his last projects, he applied his ideas about planes to boats. The result was the hydrofoil, a boat that "flew" just above the water at up to 70 miles per hour.

Hydrofoil

It's a Fact
Bell came up with the original idea for the metal detector that is used in airports.

★—☆—☆ THOMAS EDISON ☆—☆—★

Thomas Alva Edison
Born February 11, 1847, in Milan, Ohio
Died October 18, 1931, in West Orange, New Jersey
Family Married Mary Stilwell; three children. Married Mina Miller; three children
Claim to Fame Inventor who created the electric lightbulb—and over 1,000 other inventions!

I t seems so easy. You flip a switch and, as if by magic, a room lights up. But it took a brilliant inventor to bring this light to the world. Make that a brilliant, hard-working inventor. As Thomas Edison said himself, "Genius is one percent inspiration and ninety-nine percent perspiration."

Thomas Edison was always a hard worker, even as a boy with poor health and hearing. In school, however, "Al" Edison had a difficult time. When he was eight, his teacher said that his mind was not quite right. This made his mother very angry and she took him out of school. From that time on, she devoted herself to being her

son's teacher. This was a lucky break for Edison, because his mother knew he was actually very smart.

One day, when Al was ten, Mrs. Edison gave him a science book. Young Edison was fascinated with the drawings and diagrams about lightning and electricity. From then on, if anyone needed to find him, it was a good bet to look in his

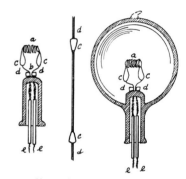

Edison's early designs for the lightbulb

basement workshop or in the "lab" he kept on the train where he sold candy and

newspapers. By the time he was 15, he was printing his own newspaper, *The Weekly Herald.*

In 1863, Edison took a job as a telegraph operator. He experimented with ways to improve the telegraph—the most important way of sending messages in those days. He

wanted to find a way to send two messages at the same time. While he was working on this challenge, he received his first patent for an electric vote-recording machine. (A patent is a legal document that protects the inventor's rights.) Edison was only 21 years old and on his way to becoming one of America's greatest inventors.

Lab in Menlo Park, New Jersey

By the age of 30, Edison had invented so many successful electrical gadgets that he had enough money to open his own research laboratory in New Jersey. It was there that he invented the lightbulb in 1879. Among Edison's later inventions were the phonograph and the motion picture camera.

The U.S. Patent Office issued 1,093 patents to Thomas Edison, many more than to any other inventor. The detailed records Edison kept of all his inventions reached nearly five million pages of notes and drawings.

It's a Fact
As a young man in a shabby telegraph office, Edison invented a device that electrocuted cockroaches!

★—★—★ SAMUEL GOMPERS ★—★—★

Samuel Gompers
Born January 27, 1850, in London, England
Died December 13, 1924, in San Antonio, Texas
Family Married Sophia Julian; six children. Married Gertrude Neuscheler
Claim to Fame Labor leader who successfully fought for better wages and conditions for American workers

Samuel Gompers came to America at the age of 13. He went to work making cigars in New York City. At that time, few workers belonged to unions. They had to work long hours for little pay. Conditions were often unsafe. Workers who protested were immediately fired.

Samuel joined the Cigar Makers' Union, a group that tried to improve working conditions for cigar makers. It wasn't long before union members went on strike. By refusing to work, they hoped to force the factory owners to make changes. But the strike failed. The workers were no better off than before.

Samuel wanted to find a way to help protect workers and their jobs. He went to work for the Federation of Organized Trades and Labor Unions and became its vice-president in 1880. Six years later, Samuel helped start the American

Federation of Labor—the AFL. He became its first president. By 1904, 1.7 million workers had joined the AFL.

Samuel Gompers's aim was to make sure that workplaces were safe and that workers' hours and wages were reasonable. He spoke out for equal treatment of all workers, regardless of race. He tried to reduce the number of strikes and the violence they sometimes caused. Because of his work, union members today have a stronger say in when and how they do their work.

It's a Fact
Today's 40-hour work week was partly Samuel Gompers's doing. 60- or 70-hour work weeks were common in the 19th century until workers organized and staged strikes.

★—★—★ GEORGE EASTMAN ★—★—★

George Eastman
Born July 12, 1854, in Waterville, New York
Died March 14, 1932, in Rochester, New York
Family One of three children
Claim to Fame Gifted inventor and businessman who made photography simple and affordable

camera back to Eastman's company for developing, printing, and reloading. In less than two years, Eastman had sold over 100,000 Kodak cameras!

In 1892, the company started making film that photographers could reload by themselves. In 1900, the company introduced the "Brownie" camera for children. It cost only one dollar.

I t seems that George Eastman was always interested in photography. He saved the money he earned as an errand boy to buy photographs and frames. As a young man, he wanted to take his own pictures. But taking photographs used to mean heavy equipment and dangerous chemicals.

Early version of camera

In 1880, the Eastman Kodak Company introduced a simple box camera called the Kodak. It was just a word that Eastman made up, but it became a very famous name. The Kodak camera took a long roll of paper film. After the film was used up, the photographers sent the entire

By 1927, Eastman Kodak produced almost all the film and cameras made in the United States. It is still one of the largest producers of photographic equipment in the world.

So by the time he was 25, Eastman worked out several ways to make it easier to take photographs. In 1880, he and Henry Strong started a photographic plate-making business in Rochester, New York. And he continued to experiment.

Eastman School of Music

It's a Fact
George Eastman was a rich and generous man. His company was the first to offer health benefits, retirement plans, and profit-sharing. He gave away $75 million to such schools as the University of Rochester (which includes the Eastman School of Music) and the Massachusetts Institute of Technology.

JANE ADDAMS

Jane Addams
Born September 6, 1860, in Cedarville, Illinois
Died May 21, 1935, in Chicago, Illinois
Family One of nine children
Claim to Fame Social worker who founded Hull House to help poor immigrant children and their families

Although Jane Addams's mother died when Jane was just two years old, her childhood was still happy. She and her father were close. She was well cared for and had an excellent education. That certainly wasn't true of many children at that time. The cities were filled with poor immigrant families, living in terrible conditions.

Jane wanted to help. She made up her mind to be a doctor, but poor health forced her to leave medical school. It took her two years to recover from an operation on her spine.

Jane didn't give up easily. She and her best friend from school decided to open a "settlement house" to help families living in one of the poorest sections of Chicago. Hull House, the first of its kind, opened its doors in 1889. Soon it included a day-care center, a kindergarten, a boarding house, a playground,

a library, a gym, meeting rooms, and a post office. When the city failed to pick up the neighborhood trash, Jane became the garbage inspector. She got up every day at dawn to be sure the job was done!

Hull House was just the beginning. Jane helped to pass laws protecting child workers. She worked to win the right to vote for women and was a founder of the NAACP, a group which fought for the rights of African Americans.

It's a Fact
In 1931, Jane Addams won the Nobel Peace Prize.

Daily Herald 2¢
DECEMBER 10, 1931
JANE ADDAMS WINS NOBEL PRIZE!
FIRST AMERICAN WOMAN TO WIN!

GEORGE W. CARVER

George Washington Carver
Born 1864, near Diamond Grove, Missouri
Died January 5, 1943, in Tuskegee, Alabama
Family Only child of slaves
Claim to Fame Scientist who developed new uses for crops, such as the peanut and sweet potato, and helped improve soil conditions for crop growing

George Washington Carver was born a slave on a small farm owned by Moses Carver. One night when George was a baby, slave raiders stole him and his mother and sold them in Arkansas.

However, Moses Carver was able to bring George back to Missouri.

As a child, Carver was small, thin, and sickly. When he noticed that some plants were small and sickly, too, he decided he should find out how to help them grow better. By the time he was seven, George was known in his Missouri town as the Plant Doctor.

The Civil War ended in 1865, and all slaves were freed. Freedom gave George the chance to go to school, where he worked very hard. He studied science at Iowa State College and did many experiments with plants. Then Tuskegee Institute, an Alabama college for African-American students, invited him to start an agricultural department to study food plants.

Peanut plant

George began experimenting with peanuts and sweet potatoes. He learned that planting peanuts helps improve the soil, so that other crops can grow better.

George Washington Carver not only taught farmers in the South how to grow better crops. He also found many new ways to use the crops southern farmers grew. He made drinks, sweeteners, and laundry starch

Student with Carver in lab

from potatoes. He made cloth and shampoo from peanuts, and also invented peanut butter and peanut flour.

When he died, Carver left his entire life savings to Tuskegee Institute. At the George Washington Carver Museum in Tuskegee, you can still see his scientific work as well as the paintings, lacework, and sculptures that he made in his spare time.

It's a Fact
George Washington Carver earned the nickname "The Wizard of Tuskegee" because he discovered over 300 products that could be made from peanuts.

TIME LINE: 1865–1899

1865 Civil War ends; Lincoln assassinated; 13th amendment to the Constitution passed, abolishing slavery.

1867 U.S. buys Alaska from Russia for $7.2 million.

1867 Wilbur Wright born in Indiana; later collaborates with his brother, Orville, to develop the first propeller airplane.

1869 Union Pacific Railroad joins Central Pacific Railroad, forming the first transcontinental railroad.

1871 Orville Wright born in Ohio.

1872 Yellowstone is named the first national park.

1874 Oscar Levi Strauss sells first pair of blue jeans.

1880 Helen Keller born in Alabama; by her own example, inspires hearing- and sight-impaired people the world over.

1881 Booker T. Washington founds Tuskegee Institute in Alabama, one of the first black colleges in America.

1883 The Brooklyn Bridge, a grand structure linking Brooklyn and Manhattan, is completed. It is the longest suspension bridge in the world.

1884 Eleanor Roosevelt born in New York; becomes First Lady in 1933 and later becomes the first American woman to serve as a delegate to the United Nations.

1886 American Federation of Labor founded.

1887 Georgia O'Keeffe born in Wisconsin; becomes one of America's best-known nature painters.

1888 Israel Baline (Irving Berlin) born in Russia; moves to America at the age of five and becomes a great songwriter. One of his most beloved songs is "God Bless America."

1894 Martha Graham born in Pennsylvania; a dancer and choreographer, she revolutionizes modern dance.

1895 George Herman (Babe) Ruth born in Maryland; in 1936, he is elected into the Baseball Hall of Fame for his great all-around playing and 714 career home runs.

1897 Amelia Earhart born in Kansas; becomes the first woman to make a solo airplane flight across the Atlantic.

THE WRIGHT BROTHERS

Wilbur and Orville Wright

Born Wilbur was born April 16, 1867, near Milville, Indiana. Orville was born August 19, 1871, in Dayton, Ohio

Died Wilbur died May 30, 1912, in Dayton, Ohio. Orville died June 30, 1948, in Dayton, Ohio

Family Two of five children of Milton and Susan Wright

Claim to Fame Inventive brothers who built the world's first propeller airplane

From an early age, Wilbur and Orville Wright seemed like twins. They shared many interests and liked to do things together. When they were young, the two boys constantly played with machines and kites.

In 1889, Wilbur wrote to the Smithsonian Institution in Washington, D.C., asking for information on flying machines. The brothers carefully studied the information. They also spent hours watching birds fly.

The Wrights' first aircraft was a glider with two wings. From wing tip to wing tip, it measured 16 feet, and it cost the brothers $15 to build. In 1900, they took it to Kitty Hawk, a small village on the Outer Banks of North Carolina. They lived in a tent on the windy dunes and tested their plane.

The Wright brothers continued improving and testing the design of their craft, adjusting the wings and adding a propeller to power the plane. Three years later, they returned

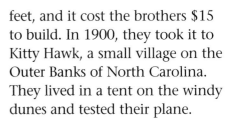

to Kitty Hawk with a larger plane, *The Flyer.* On December 17, with Orville as pilot, *The Flyer* took off. Only 12 seconds later, it crashed. But Orville had made the first motorized, controlled flight in history.

The Wrights continued to have success with their planes. It took only until 1911 for them to make the first coast-to-coast trip across the United States.

The Flyer

As adults, the brothers set up a bicycle shop in Dayton, Ohio. They sold, rented, and repaired bikes and also designed new models. The money they made from the bicycle shop helped them devote time to their dream of building a flying machine.

It's a Fact
Wilbur and Orville got many of their early ideas for airplanes from watching vultures fly.

Helen Keller
Born June 27, 1880, in Tuscumbia, Alabama
Died June 1, 1968, in Westport, Connecticut
Family One of five children
Claim to Fame Deaf and blind writer who found a way to communicate and helped thousands of others who were hearing- and sight-disabled

When Helen Keller was 19 months old, a terrible sickness left her deaf, blind, and unable to learn to speak. She was locked in a world of silent darkness until she was seven. That year, Anne Sullivan, a teacher, came to live with her.

Nearly blind herself, Anne had learned a manual alphabet—a system of forming letters with various hand positions. She tried to teach Helen the alphabet by spelling words into her hand while having her touch the objects Anne named. While trying to spell *water* into Helen's hand,

Anne ran cold water over Helen's other hand. After several months of work with Anne, Helen suddenly understood. *Water* was the cold, wet stuff she felt! A world of words opened to her, and she learned quickly.

With Anne as her friend and teacher, Helen learned to "hear" by feeling a speaker's lips, and also to speak. She mastered

Helen reading in Braille

reading and writing in Braille, a system of raised dots that people can feel with their fingertips. After graduating with honors from Radcliffe College, she began educating the public about the rights and skills of handicapped people. She toured the country, raising money for the American Foundation for the Blind, and wrote books about her experiences. During World War II, Helen helped teach soldiers who had been blinded in battle how to live without sight.

Helen Keller's courage and endurance showed people who had lost their sight and hearing that they, too, could lead productive lives.

It's a Fact
Helen Keller learned to read and speak not only English, but also French, German, Italian, and Latin.

★~~☆ ELEANOR ROOSEVELT ★~~★ ★

Anna Eleanor Roosevelt
Born October 31, 1884, in New York, New York
Died November 7, 1962, in New York, New York
Family Married Franklin Delano Roosevelt; five surviving children
Claim to Fame First Lady and United Nations delegate who crusaded for peace and human rights

Eleanor Roosevelt was born into a rich family, but she did not have a happy childhood. In a family of very beautiful and lively women, Eleanor was a plain and shy little girl. Her mother's family told her over and over again how awkward and ugly they thought she was. Eleanor's father was kinder to her, but he had personal problems that kept him from spending much time with her. By the time she was ten, both her parents were dead. Eleanor moved in with her grandmother, two aunts, and two uncles.

Eleanor was very shy. With the help of her teachers at a girls' boarding school in England, she became more outgoing. By the time she married Franklin Delano Roosevelt, her fifth cousin, in 1905, she was ready for an active public life. And that's certainly what the Roosevelts had. Franklin later became governor of New York and then President of the United States.

Partly because Franklin suffered from polio, an illness which left him unable to walk,

Eleanor at boarding school

Eleanor was a very active First Lady. She had her own varied career as a magazine columnist, lecturer, and spokesperson for children, minorities, and the poor. She was constantly on the go, traveling 40,000 miles during her first year in the White House.

During World War II, Eleanor represented the White House on her many trips to Europe. She even visited soldiers in the South Pacific. She wanted them to be able to see the First Lady in person

and to know that everyone at home supported them.

After Franklin died in 1945, Eleanor devoted most of her time to working toward world peace as a delegate to the United Nations. Mrs. Roosevelt, who as a child was made to feel that "nothing about me would attract attention or bring me admiration," was voted Most Admired Woman of 1948.

It's a Fact
Eleanor Roosevelt was the first First Lady to travel in an airplane.

GEORGIA O'KEEFFE

Georgia O'Keeffe
Born November 15, 1887, in Sun Prairie, Wisconsin
Died March 6, 1986, in Santa Fe, New Mexico
Family Married Alfred Stieglitz
Claim to Fame Artist who painted eye-catching, often enormous pictures of flowers, bones, and other objects from nature, especially from the desert

Georgia O'Keeffe grew up on a farm with four sisters and two brothers. She always loved the outdoors. She had a strong mind and her own ideas. At a time when girls didn't do such things, Georgia would grab the reins and drive the horse and buggy to church. While other girls wore fancy dresses, she wanted only plain ones.

Georgia could draw beautifully, so her parents sent her to art school in Chicago. She also studied at several other schools. Afterward she taught art in Texas, where she took her students outdoors to draw weeds, rocks, and sun-bleached cattle bones scattered around the shimmering desert. Georgia wanted to help them see the beauty all around them.

All this time O'Keeffe continued with her own paintings. Her work featured the

same kinds of objects from nature that she displayed for her students. She used clear colors and lines in her paintings. When she painted her famous, dazzling giant flowers, one art critic said Georgia wanted people to feel as if they were butterflies, about to land on the petals.

Not everyone liked Georgia's work. Some people were shocked that a woman would create such bold paintings. But most art lovers now consider the artist, who lived to the age of 98, to be a genius.

It's a Fact
Georgia O'Keeffe liked big paintings. Her work "Sky Above Clouds IV" is more than 20 feet wide. She painted it in sections and stored the work in an airplane hangar.

Irving Berlin
Born May 11, 1888, in Mohilev, Russia
Died September 22, 1989, in New York, New York
Family Married Dorothy Goetz. Married Ellin Mackay; four children
Claim to Fame Songwriter who composed some of the most famous popular songs of the 20th century

During some parts of his life, Berlin wrote three new songs a day! His first big hit was "Alexander's Ragtime Band."

Two of Irving Berlin's most famous songs are "White Christmas" and "Easter Parade." Although he didn't grow up celebrating these holidays, his neighborhood was filled with immigrants from many different

Israel "Izzy" Baline was five years old when his family left Russia and came to the United States. In Russia at that time, Jewish people like the Balines had few rights. They could not work at some jobs, they could live only in certain places, and they were the targets of *pogroms*—mass killings.

The Balines lived in poverty in a tiny, crowded New York City apartment. But there was always bright, wonderful music. Izzy's father was a cantor, the chief singer at Jewish religious services. Cantor Baline loved to sing around the house, too, and his young son often joined in.

Because his family was so poor, Izzy left home and school at age 14 to earn money. The years of singing with his father came in handy when he got a job as a singing waiter. After a while he changed his name to Irving Berlin and went from *singing* songs to *writing* them. And once he got started, he just kept going.

countries, and he loved all kinds of celebrations.

Irving Berlin wrote more than 1,500 songs, including "God Bless America." His gentle, upbeat music helped Americans cope with the sad years of the Great Depression and World War II.

It's a Fact
Irving Berlin could not read music and played the piano on the black keys only.

MARTHA GRAHAM

Martha Graham
Born May 11, 1894, in Allegheny County, Pennsylvania
Died April 1, 1991, in New York, New York
Family Married Eric Hawkins
Claim to Fame Dancer and choreographer who created modern dance

Martha soon began to choreograph—create her own dances. They were different from the popular ballets of the time. She found fresh ideas in history, Bible stories, and Native American and Greek legends. They were rich with emotion. She wanted her dances to make people think and feel.

When Martha Graham was growing up, dance was not considered a serious art form in the United States. There was little professional dance outside of variety shows. Isadora Duncan and Ruth St. Denis, however, became famous for their classical solo dances. Martha knew she wanted to be a dancer like them. She studied dance with St. Denis in California, and in 1923, she moved to New York City to live her dream.

Martha opened her own school of dance in 1951. She kept choreographing, designing 191 dances in all. Her company toured all over Europe and the Middle East. It was the first dance company to include African-American and Asian-American dancers. Even today, Martha Graham's school and company still produce great dancers and dances.

The work of Martha Graham changed the dance world. What is now called modern dance began with her. She herself continued dancing until 1970, giving her last performance at the age of 75. And she kept creating dances until she was 96 years old!

It's a Fact
Martha Graham performed for eight presidents of the United States. President Gerald Ford awarded her the Presidential Medal of Freedom, the country's highest civilian honor, in 1976.

Martha dancing solo in Aztec costume

BABE RUTH

Babe Ruth
Born February 6, 1895, in Baltimore, Maryland
Died August 16, 1948, in New York, New York
Family Married Helen Woodford; one child. Married Claire Merritt
Claim to Fame Baseball player who has been called the greatest in the history of the game

great hitting that he wanted him to play every day. So Babe stopped pitching and played in the outfield.

Babe changed the game of baseball. Before he came to the Major Leagues, players rarely hit more than three or four home runs in a season. Babe's pitching experience helped him as a hitter, and his great strength

When George Herman Ruth was growing up, he was a tough street kid who was always in trouble. In fact, when he was seven years old, his parents put him in a reform school, hoping he would learn how to stay out of trouble.

At the school, a priest named Brother Matthias took a special liking to young George. Brother

Matthias loved baseball and taught George to play. George became an excellent hitter and pitcher. In 1914, the owner of a minor-league team saw him play and invited him to join the team.

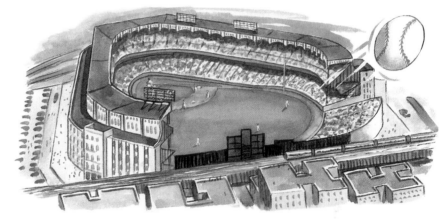

George was the youngest player on the team, so the older players started calling him "Babe." And it stuck with him for the rest of his life.

Babe pitched for the Boston Red Sox for six seasons. Then, in 1920, he joined the New York Yankees. The Yankees' manager was so impressed with Babe's

blasted the ball over the fences. Babe hit 30, 40, 50 home runs every year. In 1927, he hit 60! This record stood for 34 years.

Babe was one of the first five players voted into the new Baseball Hall of Fame in 1936. Because of his records and his star quality, he has remained the most famous player of all.

It's a Fact
Fans loved Babe for his outgoing personality, as well as his exciting play. Babe was very generous to his many young fans. He loved spending time with them and signing autographs.

AMELIA EARHART

Amelia Earhart
Born July 24, 1897, in Atchison, Kansas
Died Last heard from somewhere over the central Pacific Ocean, July 2, 1937
Family Married George Putnam
Claim to Fame Aviator who was the first woman to cross the Atlantic Ocean alone in a plane

Amelia Earhart always liked machines. When she was six, she invented a chicken trap. It caught the chickens that were always escaping from her neighbor's yard. Later, she built a roller coaster in her own backyard. Even so, young Amelia would probably have been surprised if she knew that someday she would pilot her own airplane.

In the early 1900s, women did not fly planes. But after watching pilots do stunts in an air circus, Amelia decided she had to learn to fly. She took lessons and by 1922 she was a skilled pilot with her own plane. She flew higher than any other woman had flown. She also had a few accidents, one time crash-landing in a cornfield. Luckily, she was unhurt.

In 1927, Charles Lindbergh made the first flight across the Atlantic Ocean. A year later, Amelia flew as a crew member from Canada to Wales, and became the first woman to cross the ocean by plane. Four years later, she flew across the Atlantic alone.

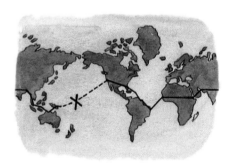

"X" shows where around-the-world flight disappeared

Amelia went on to set more flying records. She also gave speeches about flying and was honored at the White House. In 1937, she set a huge challenge for herself: she would fly around the entire world. Amelia and her navigator, Fred Noonan, set off from Miami, Florida. After they had flown 22,000 miles, about three-quarters of their trip, their plane disappeared over the Pacific Ocean on July 2, 1937. Neither one was ever seen again.

It's a Fact
Amelia Earhart once sneaked out of a party with First Lady Eleanor Roosevelt and took her on a night flight. Both women were wearing evening dresses!

TIME LINE: 1900–1918

1900 L. Frank Baum publishes *The Wizard of Oz.*

1901 Walt Disney born in Illinois; creates memorable cartoon characters and animated films.

1901 Margaret Mead born in Pennsylvania; a noted anthropologist, she specializes in Pacific Island cultures.

1902 Langston Hughes born in Missouri; celebrates African-American life and culture in his stories and poems.

1902 First appearance of Crayola crayons.

1902 Marian Anderson born in Pennsylvania; becomes the first African American to perform at the Metropolitan Opera House in New York.

1903 First World Series (Boston Red Sox defeat Pittsburgh Pirates).

1906 A huge earthquake rocks San Francisco, destroying two-thirds of the city.

1908 Thurgood Marshall born in Maryland; in 1967, becomes the first African American to sit on the U.S. Supreme Court.

1908 Henry Ford introduces the Model T, the world's first moderately priced car.

1909 Admiral Robert E. Peary reaches the North Pole, becoming the first person to stand on "the roof of the world."

1911 Lucille Ball born in New York; becomes one of TV's most popular actresses.

1912 The *Titanic* sinks on its maiden voyage.

1913 Rosa McCauley (Parks) born in Alabama; challenges the practice of segregation.

1913 Jesse Owens born in Alabama; in 1936, wins gold medals in track and field at the Berlin Olympics.

1914 Panama Canal opens, connecting the Atlantic and Pacific Oceans.

1914 Jonas Salk born in New York; in 1952, discovers the cure for polio.

1917 United States enters World War I.

1917 I. M. Pei born in China; comes to America to attend college and becomes a great architect.

1918 Pauline and Esther Friedman (Abigail Van Buren/Ann Landers) born in Iowa; team up to write advice columns that are later syndicated in newspapers around the world.

1918 An influenza epidemic causes the deaths of more than 20 million people worldwide, including over half a million Americans.

WALT DISNEY

Walt Disney
Born December 5, 1901, in Chicago, Illinois
Died December 15, 1966, in Los Angeles, California
Family Married Lillian Bounds; two children
Claim to Fame Cartoonist who created timeless characters and theme parks known the world over

The Disney family knew very early that Walt had a great imagination. He spent his early years on a farm, where he gave the animals names like Porky the pig, Martha the hen, and Rupert the horse. Animals such as these would soon turn up in some of the world's best-loved cartoons.

Young Walt loved to draw, and kept practicing and developing his talent. He moved to Kansas City and tried to get a job as a cartoonist for a newspaper, without success. But Walt got his first break working for an advertising company that made cartoons on film. Cartoon filmmaking, often called animation, was a new business. When Walt realized that the future of movie cartoons was in Hollywood, he moved to California.

He opened an animation studio with his brother Roy. It was there that he and artist Ub Iwerks created Mickey Mouse.

His first Mickey Mouse film, *Steamboat Willie*, was the first cartoon with sound. In fact, Walt spoke Mickey's dialogue on the sound track! Mickey and Walt became huge stars.

Walt Disney went on to make many short and feature-length cartoons. *The Three Little Pigs, Snow White, Dumbo,* and *Bambi* are some of his best-known films. In the 1950s, he began building Disneyland, in California. In the first two months, over a million people visited the theme park. Today, there are Disney parks near Orlando, Florida, in Tokyo, Japan, and outside Paris, France. People all over the world enjoy the wonderful characters and stories that Walt Disney created.

It's a Fact
Mickey Mouse's original name was Mortimer, but Lillian Disney made her husband change it. She thought Mortimer was just not catchy enough.

Disneyland

Margaret Mead
Born December 16, 1901, in Philadelphia, Pennsylvania
Died November 15, 1978, in New York, New York
Family Married Luther Cressman. Married Reo Fortune. Married Gregory Bateson; one child
Claim to Fame Anthropologist who studied and wrote about Pacific Island cultures and popularized the field of anthropology

Margaret later worked at the American Museum of Natural History in New York City. She continued to study and write about several South Sea Island cultures. World War II interrupted her work, and when she went back to the islands, she found that the cultures had changed. Modern medicine and technology had arrived. So, Margaret wrote about how modern life changes cultures.

Margaret Mead grew up in a family that cared deeply about learning. Her grandmother urged her to study science. Margaret also kept charts that showed her younger sisters' growth and development. This work taught Margaret to watch, listen, and write about people's actions.

23, she went to the island of Samoa. There, she lived among the Samoan people and studied them, especially the girls. She wrote *Coming of Age in Samoa* about her experiences, and it became a best-selling book.

Because of Margaret Mead's work, anthropology became a popular science. Margaret helped people learn about differences and similarities among the peoples of the world. She showed that the more we understand each other, the better we can get along.

After attending Columbia University, Margaret became an anthropologist. She studied human cultures and was especially interested in the South Sea Islands. When she was only

American Museum of Natural History

It's a Fact
When Margaret Mead went to Samoa, she had to learn to eat Samoan food: eel, green bananas, raw fish, and bat.

★LANGSTON HUGHES★

Langston Hughes
Born February 1, 1902, in Joplin, Missouri
Died May 22, 1967, in New York, New York
Family Raised by his grandmother
Claim to Fame Writer who is known especially for his poetry on African-American life

Langston Hughes lived with his grandmother most of the time he was growing up. She was a loving woman who told Langston wonderful stories and encouraged him to read books. The boy loved to read and write. When he was 14, his classmates voted him Class Poet. Langston decided he would make writing his life's work.

In fact, Langston Hughes had his first poem published just after he graduated from high school. He kept writing during the next several years as he traveled through Mexico, Africa, and Europe.

When Langston returned from his travels, he worked in a Washington, D.C., hotel. One night, he noticed the famous poet Vachel Lindsay, having dinner. Langston was too shy to speak to Lindsay, but he left some of his poems beside Lindsay's plate. Lindsay was surprised. But he found the young man to be so talented that he helped find a publisher for Langston's first book of poetry.

Soon, Langston's poems began to win prizes. He also began to write plays, novels, stories, and articles. In the 1930s, he helped to start an African-American theater company and to publish collections of African-American writing. He also began traveling all over the country, lecturing and reading his poetry.

Langston Hughes's writing often focused on the challenges of African-American life. With rhythms from jazz and blues, his poems have a lively musical quality; they touch people's minds and hearts. His poem "Hope" runs:

Sometimes when I'm lonely,
Don't know why,
Keep thinkin' I won't be lonely
By and by.

It's a Fact
Langston Hughes did not want his funeral to be sad. His friends respected his wishes and played music and read his poetry aloud at the service.

Langston reading his poetry

★≻★≺★ MARIAN ANDERSON ★≻★≺★

Marian Anderson
Born February 17, 1902, in Philadelphia, Pennsylvania
Died April 8, 1993, in Portland, Oregon
Family Married Orpheus Fisher
Claim to Fame African-American singer who was one of the greatest concert and opera performers

From the time she was a toddler, Marian Anderson loved to sing. She began singing in a church choir at age six. She learned all the parts to the songs the choir sang. That way, if anyone was sick, Marian could sing his or her part.

Marian studied classical music seriously and her beautiful voice grew stronger and more mature. At the age of 19 she sang at Town Hall in New York City, but the concert did not go well, and she got poor reviews. She almost gave up singing right then, but she decided to work even harder and to improve.

Three years later, Marian sang again in New York. This time she was a great success. Because

African Americans had few opportunities in the United States at this time, Marian made many trips to Europe, where she studied, performed, and became famous.

In 1939, Marian was to appear at Constitution Hall, a famous concert hall in Washington, D.C. But she was told she couldn't sing there because she was an

African American. First Lady Eleanor Roosevelt stood up for her and spoke against prejudice. With Mrs. Roosevelt's help, Marian Anderson gave her concert after all—on the steps of the Lincoln Memorial. An audience of 75,000 people cheered for her. Later she became the first African American to sing with the Metropolitan Opera Company of New York.

In the 1950s, President Dwight Eisenhower made Marian a delegate to the United Nations. She sang the national anthem at President John F. Kennedy's inauguration in 1961. President Lyndon Johnson gave her the Presidential Medal of Freedom. Marian Anderson once said, "I wasn't a great fighter. I hope that my work will speak."

It's a Fact
Marian Anderson's mother worked as a cleaning woman at a department store to earn the money to pay for Marian's singing lessons. Marian said later that her happiest moment was the day her mother quit.

★ THURGOOD MARSHALL ★

Thurgood Marshall
Born July 2, 1908, in Baltimore, Maryland
Died January 24, 1993, in Bethesda, Maryland
Family Married Vivian Burey. Married Cecilia Suyat; two children
Claim to Fame Civil rights lawyer who was the first African-American member of the United States Supreme Court

As a boy, Thurgood Marshall was a good student, but he often got into trouble. As punishment, his teachers made him memorize parts of the U.S. Constitution. Little did he know he would spend his life studying that document!

Thurgood went to law school, and then set up his own law practice, at which he was very successful. Still, he often struggled to make ends meet because so many of his clients were poor.

Later, Marshall worked as a lawyer for the National Association for the Advancement of Colored People (NAACP). At that time, people in the United States were largely segregated—separated by race. In some states, certain schools, hotels—even water fountains—were for white people only. Thurgood wanted to end segregation.

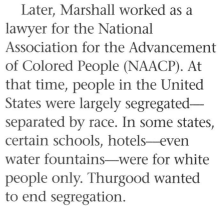

He won many lawsuits that allowed African Americans to go to white schools and colleges. In one of the most important cases, *Brown v. Board of Education*, the U.S. Supreme Court—the country's highest court—agreed with Thurgood that keeping black students out of public schools was against the law under the Constitution.

In 1967, President Lyndon Johnson appointed Thurgood to that very court. He was the first African-American Supreme Court Justice. On the court, he was a champion for equal rights for all.

We the people of the United States of America...

It's a Fact
Thurgood Marshall's name came from his great-grandfather, a slave named Thoroughgood.

Lucille Ball
Born August 6, 1911, in Celoron, New York
Died April 26, 1989, in Los Angeles, California
Family Married Desi Arnaz; two children. Married Gary Morton
Claim to Fame Comedian who was one of the most beloved, best-known early TV stars

At 15, Lucille Ball dropped out of high school to go to drama school in New York City. She found work as a model, and soon after she went to Hollywood, where she landed several small parts in movies. When she was cast in a movie with the handsome Cuban singer and bandleader Desi Arnaz, they

fell in love and soon married. In the late 1940s, Lucille starred in a radio show called *My Favorite Husband,* playing the scatterbrained wife of a Midwestern banker.

The show was very popular with audiences, and Lucille got an offer to star in a television version of it. Television was a new form of home entertainment, and the move was risky, but Lucille agreed to try it if they would cast Desi as her husband. The Midwestern

banker was rewritten to become a Cuban musician, and the new show, called *I Love Lucy,* was a hit.

Lucille took no screen credit for directing or writing *I Love Lucy,* but she was the star and was very much in charge of the show. She created many of the show's funniest moments. She also insisted that her character, Lucy Ricardo, remain a middle-class housewife with the same kinds of problems as most of her audience had—fixing a broken washing machine or paying for a new coat. The show was a huge success and remains popular with new generations of fans through reruns.

Lucy, Desi, and their TV neighbors, Ethel and Fred

It's a Fact
On January 19, 1953, almost three-quarters of all the TV sets in the United States were tuned to a special episode in which Lucy's TV son, Ricky Ricardo, Jr., was born. In real life, Lucille Ball delivered her son, Desi Arnaz IV, on the same day.

Rosa McCauley Parks
Born February 4, 1913, in Tuskegee, Alabama
Family Married Raymond Parks
Claim to Fame Granddaughter of slaves, she began the Montgomery, Alabama, Bus Boycott by refusing to give up her seat on a bus

On December 1, 1955, in Montgomery, Alabama, Rosa was riding the Cleveland Avenue bus home. She was tired from working all day, but more important, she was tired of segregation. When a white man boarded the crowded bus and wanted her seat, she refused to get up. The driver called the police, and Rosa was arrested.

When Rosa McCauley was growing up in Alabama, African Americans were segregated—kept apart—from whites. They could not live in white neighborhoods, go to white schools, hold many kinds of jobs, or eat in certain restaurants. They had to sit in the back of buses and give up their seats if white people wanted them. Rosa hated segregation, but it was the law in the South.

In 1943, Rosa joined the National Association for the Advancement of Colored People (NAACP). There she learned about ways to challenge the laws of segregation and to work toward overcoming unequal treatment of African Americans.

To help Rosa, and to change the law, the African Americans of Montgomery refused to ride the city buses. This boycott lasted for a whole year. Then the U.S. Supreme Court, the country's highest court, ruled that segregation on public buses was illegal. Rosa had won!

But the people who wanted to keep segregation made Rosa pay for her victory. Rosa and her husband, Raymond, both lost their jobs. They moved to Detroit. There they started the Rosa and Raymond Parks Institute for Self-Development. The Institute teaches young people how to work to change unfair things in our country. Rosa's work helped the Civil Rights Movement tremendously. Her courage helped show all Americans that everyone deserves the same rights.

It's a Fact
Cleveland Avenue in Montgomery, Alabama, was later renamed. It is now called Rosa Parks Boulevard.

JESSE OWENS

Jesse Owens
Born September 12, 1913, in Danville, Alabama
Died March 31, 1980, in Phoenix, Arizona
Family Married Ruth Solomon; three children
Claim to Fame Track-and-field star who won four gold medals in the 1936 Olympics in Berlin

heritage were stronger and better than everyone else. He expected the German athletes to prove this with Olympic victories.

Jesse was the star of the games, winning the 100-meter dash, the 200-meter dash, and the running broad jump. He was also part of the record-breaking 400-meter relay team.

James Cleveland Owens's father was a poor farm worker who moved his family from Alabama to Ohio in search of a better life. Jesse got his nickname when a teacher asked his name, and he answered with his initials, "J.C." Because of his Southern accent, she thought he had said "Jesse."

The Owens family had no money to spend on amusements, so, for fun, Jesse ran. At 13, he began competing in races, and soon he was also doing the running broad jump (now called the long jump) and the high jump. He worked his way through Ohio State University as a waiter and a night-elevator operator, still finding the time

to train and compete. He won meet after meet and attracted national attention.

In 1936, he took his talents to the Summer Olympics in Berlin, Germany. Adolf Hitler was Germany's dictator. Hitler believed that people of German

An angry Hitler snubbed him and refused to shake his hand because he was black. Twenty years later, Owens attended the 1956 Olympics in Melbourne, Australia, as President Dwight Eisenhower's personal representative.

It's a Fact
Jesse Owens started an orchestra, appeared in a Hollywood film, and ran and won a race against a horse in Cuba!

★ JONAS SALK ★

Jonas Salk
Born October 28, 1914, in New York, New York
Died June 23, 1995, in La Jolla, California
Family Married Donna Lindsay; three children. Married Françoise Gilot
Claim to Fame Research physician who developed vaccines for influenza and polio

University's School of Medicine. Next, Dr. Salk went to work at the University of Michigan, where he and another doctor, Thomas Francis, Jr., developed a vaccine for a type of flu. They found that injecting people with dead flu viruses prevented them from getting the disease. This was a very important breakthrough in medicine.

In 1916, when Jonas Salk was only two years old, many cases of the disease called poliomyelitis, or polio, broke out across the country. This disease affected many children and some adults. Many of them died. Others became paralyzed. Jonas did not get polio, but he spent most of his medical career studying the dreaded disease. He wanted to find a way to protect people from the virus.

Jonas was always a hard-working student. He entered college when he was only 15, and attended New York

In 1947, Dr. Salk began working on a polio vaccine. In five years, he had successfully developed one. In the mid-1950s, the "Salk vaccine" was given to thousands of American schoolchildren. Dr. Salk quickly became an American hero.

In 1963, Dr. Salk moved to California, where he worked at the Institute for Biological Studies. It later became the Salk Institute, a place where scientists work together and exchange ideas. In 1977, Salk was awarded the Presidential Medal of Freedom. In later years, he tried to develop a vaccine for the virus that causes AIDS.

It's a Fact
During the polio epidemic of 1916, parents were afraid to let their children go to movie theaters, public libraries, or even churches.

☆ I. M. PEI ☆

I. M. Pei
Born April 26, 1917, in Canton, China
Family Married Eileen Loo; four children
Claim to Fame Talented architect who designed some of the greatest buildings of the 20th century

Ieoh Ming Pei was born to a family that expected great things from its children. Pei is the 15th generation of a wealthy family of gifted poets, artists, and bankers. In fact, *Ieoh Ming* means "to write brightly." This shows what his parents hoped for in their first son. He was born in the Year of the Snake, which many Chinese believe gives a child great charm and strength of mind.

In the part of China where Pei grew up, many rich families had a special kind of house, or retreat. The retreat was richly decorated and had beautiful, quiet gardens. Families met there for poetry readings, art exhibits, and lessons with private tutors. The Pei family's retreat was called "Garden of the Lion Forest." Strong memories of the

wonderful retreat stayed with Pei his whole life. He often thought back to it to help him come up with his own designs.

It was common for wealthy Chinese parents to send their children to Europe or the United States for college. Pei ended up at the Massachusetts Institute of

Pei's pyramid at The Louvre, Paris

Technology, where he studied engineering. But an architecture professor, feeling that Pei had great artistic talent, convinced him to change his field. When he graduated, World War II kept him from returning to China, so he stayed in the States. He worked at several architecture firms, where he and his wonderful designs grew famous. He formed his own company in 1955 and designed many remarkable buildings in the U.S., Europe, and China. His buildings are known for their exciting shapes and spaces. One example is the East Building of Washington, D.C.'s National Gallery of Art, a striking and spacious structure of triangular spaces.

It's a Fact
When Pei first came to the United States, he studied architecture at the University of Pennsylvania. But he dropped out after only two weeks because he didn't think that he drew as well as some other students.

Abigail Van Buren (Pauline Esther Friedman)
Ann Landers (Esther Pauline Friedman)
Born July 4, 1918, in Sioux City, Iowa
Family Abigail Van Buren: Married Mort Phillips; two children.
Ann Landers: Married Jules Lederer; one child
Claim to Fame Identical twins who have identical jobs—writing advice columns that appear in newspapers all over the world

It seems fitting that America's most famous twins were born on the Fourth of July. Esther Pauline, or "Eppie," was born first. Pauline Esther, or "Popo," arrived 17 minutes later. Growing up, the two girls did almost everything together. They went to the same college. They even had a double wedding!

Eppie got her start as an advice columnist by winning a contest. The woman who had been writing the "Ann Landers" column for the *Chicago Sun Times* died. The newspaper was searching for someone to replace her. Eppie gave the editors 40 sample columns. Her thoughtful solutions to people's problems impressed the contest judges. Though she'd never worked as a writer before, Eppie got the job.

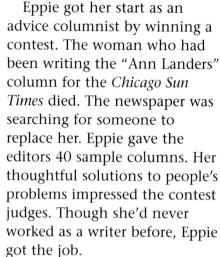

Popo became "Dear Abby" not long after. She had been helping Eppie with her column. That gave her the confidence to try writing one by herself. The *San Francisco Chronicle* editors hired Popo because of her short and sometimes funny answers to readers' problems.

The Ann Landers and Dear Abby columns are printed in more than 2,000 newspapers. They are read by nearly 200 million people.

It's a Fact
Popo signs her "Dear Abby" column Abigail Van Buren—after Martin Van Buren, the eighth President of the United States.

★—★—★ CESAR CHAVEZ ★—★—★

Cesar Chavez
Born March 31, 1927, near Yuma, Arizona
Died April 22, 1993, in San Luis, Arizona
Family Married Helen Fabela; eight children
Claim to Fame Mexican-American labor leader who led peaceful protests and hunger strikes to improve the working conditions of migrant farm workers

National Farm Workers Association (NFWA), to protect the rights of migrant workers. NFWA drew the attention of people across the country when it supported a strike by grape pickers. They had been forced to work in scorching heat and come into contact with poisonous chemicals used to kill insects.

During his life, Cesar helped organize many farm workers.

When Cesar Chavez was ten years old, something happened that changed his life. His parents had to give up their own farm and become migrant workers—workers who moved from farm to farm picking crops. Even with the whole family

working, the Chavez family often earned as little as one dollar for a day's work. They lived in run-down shacks with no bathroom or kitchen. These were the conditions most migrant workers had to accept. Cesar grew up determined to improve migrant workers' lives.

As an adult, Cesar began talking to other migrant workers

and encouraged them to fight for their rights. He had learned of Indian political leader Mahatma Ghandi's ideas of peaceful resistance, and applied these ideas in the Southwest. He helped workers register to vote, and taught them how to organize to get better treatment.

In 1962, Cesar and his wife, Helen, formed a labor union, the

Three times he went on hunger strikes—he stopped eating—as a dramatic way of telling the world about the migrant workers' harsh life. Cesar's protests finally got the government to take action. In 1975, California passed the Agricultural Labor Relations Act, a bill of rights for farm workers—the first in the United States.

It's a Fact
In one of Chavez's most famous speeches he said: "The truest act of courage… is to sacrifice ourselves for others in a totally nonviolent struggle for justice."

Maya Angelou (Marguerite Johnson)
Born April 4, 1928, in St. Louis, Missouri
Family Married Tosh Angelos. Married Vusumi Make; one child
Claim to Fame Poet, playwright, performer, and teacher who has written and performed many inspirational works, often about the African-American experience

When Marguerite Johnson was only eight years old, something terrible happened to her. She was attacked by a friend of the family. The man was caught, but for a long time afterward Marguerite stayed silent. She wouldn't speak a word to anyone except her brother, Bailey. Marguerite found another way to express her painful feelings. She started writing poetry and keeping journals.

Later, Marguerite went to San Francisco and supported herself by singing and dancing. She was so talented that the producers of an opera, *Porgy and Bess,* asked her to dance and tour with the company.

In 1957, Marguerite moved to New York, where she joined a group of talented young writers in the Harlem Writers' Club. She also worked in the Civil Rights Movement.

Marguerite began publishing her writing. She used the name Maya Angelou; Maya was Bailey's nickname for her and

Angelou was an altered spelling of her husband's name. She wrote about African traditions in American life for National Public Television. She published and recorded her poetry. She also wrote several books about her life, including *I Know Why the Caged Bird Sings.* In 1993, President Bill Clinton honored her by inviting her to deliver a new poem at his inauguration.

Maya Angelou describes her work this way: "I speak to the black experience, but I am always talking about the human condition, about what we can endure, dream, fail, and still survive."

It's a Fact
Maya Angelou won an Emmy nomination for her acting role in the TV miniseries *Roots.* It was based on the book by Alex Haley in which he traces his family back to Africa.

⭐—⭐—⭐ JAMES WATSON ⭐—⭐—⭐

James Watson
Born April 6, 1928, in Chicago, Illinois
Family Married Elizabeth Lewis; two children
Claim to Fame Scientist who was awarded the Nobel Prize for the discovery of the molecular structure of DNA

Jim Watson was still a college student when he decided to solve a great mystery. He wanted to figure out how genes—bits of information in the cells of animals and plants—work. At that time, some scientists believed that the chemical known as DNA (deoxyribonucleic acid) carried information from generation to generation.

In his early twenties, with a degree in zoology (the study of animals), Dr. Watson sailed to Europe to work at Cambridge University in England. There he met Francis Crick, a British scientist who was also interested in solving the mystery of genes.

Both men were convinced that DNA carried the information to create a plant or animal. They believed that if they could learn more about DNA, they would unravel more of the mystery. Then Watson had an idea: maybe discovering

DNA double-helix molecule

how DNA looked would help them understand how it worked. He and Crick began working together and found that DNA is shaped like two winding spiral pieces of thread—a shape called a double helix.

In 1962, Watson, Crick, and another scientist, Maurice Wilkins, were awarded a Nobel Prize for their work. The information they discovered about DNA has led to some of the most important scientific work in this century. Watson's research has helped scientists understand how traits are inherited, find ways to prevent some genetic diseases, and clone plants and animals.

It's a Fact
There is a huge model of DNA at Epcot Center at Disney World in Florida.

★ ☆ MARTIN LUTHER KING, JR. ☆ ★

Martin Luther King, Jr.
Born January 15, 1929, in Atlanta, Georgia
Died April 4, 1968, in Memphis, Tennessee
Family Married Coretta Scott; four children
Claim to Fame Civil rights leader whose words about love and peace inspired Americans to protest racial discrimination

Young Martin was a very bright boy. He learned to read before he even started school. Throughout his school years, he was interested in the ideas of great people who had helped bring about social change peacefully.

Martin saw much around him that needed to be changed.

Although slavery had ended nearly 70 years before he was born, African Americans had never been given the full rights of free citizens. They were often denied education, good jobs, comfortable modern housing, or even such basics as the use of public bathrooms and water fountains. This was especially true in the South, where Martin lived.

Martin became a minister in Montgomery, Alabama, in 1954. He took part in some important protests for the civil

rights of African Americans in Alabama. He always advised peaceful methods.

Later, Dr. King led many more peaceful protests and sit-ins against whites-only waiting rooms, lunch counters, and restrooms. And he led marches for freedom, including the historic march of more than 250,000 people in Washington, D.C., in 1963. That day Dr. King made his most famous

speech, known afterwards as "I Have a Dream." He talked about his vision of an America where all people live together in peace and friendship.

On April 4, 1968, Dr. King went to Memphis, Tennessee, to march on behalf of African-American garbage workers. As he stood on the balcony outside his motel room, Dr. King was shot and killed.

In 1964, Dr. King was awarded the Nobel Peace Prize for his civil rights work. Today, we celebrate his birthday as a national holiday.

It's a Fact
Martin Luther King dreamed of freedom for all Americans. The stone that marks his grave says: "Free at last. Thank God Almighty I'm free at last."

56

SANDRA DAY O'CONNOR

Sandra Day O'Connor
Born March 26, 1930, in El Paso, Texas
Family Married John O'Connor; three children
Claim to Fame First woman to be named a Justice of the United States Supreme Court

position of majority leader of the Arizona State Senate. In 1974, she was elected judge of the Arizona Superior Court, and in 1979, she was appointed to the Arizona Court of Appeals. As a judge, Sandra quickly became known for her intelligence.

On September 25, 1981, President Ronald Reagan appointed Sandra Day O'Connor the 102nd

S andra's parents ran a cattle ranch in Arizona called the Lazy B. As a young girl, Sandra learned how to ride a horse, drive a tractor, and brand cattle. She loved the ranch, but her parents wanted her to attend good schools. So she lived with her grandparents in Texas during the school year.

After college, Sandra attended law school at Stanford University in California. She graduated at

the top of her class. But at that time, it was very difficult for a woman to get work as a lawyer. Sandra spent the early part of her career raising her three sons and doing volunteer work.

Then, in 1965, Sandra was hired as an assistant attorney general for the state of Arizona. Four years later, she became the first woman elected to the

Supreme Court justice. She became the first woman appointed to the most important court in the nation.

It's a Fact
In 1949, when Justice O'Connor began law school, many law schools in the United States didn't even admit women as students. At the beginning of the 20th century, women weren't allowed to practice law in the United States.

★—★—☆ NEIL ARMSTRONG ★—★—★

Neil Armstrong
Born August 5, 1930, in Wapakoneta, Ohio
Family Married Janet Shearon; two children
Claim to Fame Astronaut who was the first person to walk on the moon

F rom the time six-year-old Neil Armstrong went for his first ride in an airplane, he was hooked on flying. He took flying lessons at 15 and got his pilot's license the next year—even before he had a license to drive a car!

Armstrong became a jet pilot for the U.S. Navy. In 1962, he joined NASA, the National Aeronautics and Space Administration. After four years of tough training, Astronaut

Armstrong was ready to fly high—right into space.

On his first mission, aboard *Gemini 8*, he docked his spaceship with a vehicle already in orbit—something no one had ever done before. But that "first" was nothing compared to what lay ahead. On his next mission, *Apollo 11*, Neil Armstrong shot for the moon.

On July 20, 1969, Armstrong and fellow astronauts Michael Collins and Buzz Aldrin smoothly set down their lunar landing craft, the *Eagle*, on the moon's dusty surface. Armstrong climbed out first, speaking the most famous words in the history of space exploration: "That's one small step for a man, one giant leap for mankind." His words were heard around the world as millions watched the spectacular event on television. The mission led by Neil Armstrong put the United States in the forefront of space exploration.

It's a Fact
Neil Armstrong and Buzz Aldrin spent 21 hours, 37 minutes on the moon, collecting samples and performing tests.

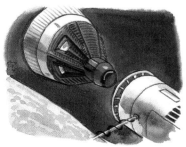
Gemini 8

Wilma Rudolph
Born June 23, 1940, in Clarksville, Tennessee
Died November 12, 1994, in Brentwood, Tennessee
Family Married Robert Eldridge; three children
Claim to Fame Athlete who overcame many obstacles to become the first American woman to win three gold medals at a single Olympics

the youngest member of the U.S. team.

Wilma and her American teammates won a bronze medal in the women's relay race. Four years later, after giving birth to a daughter and starting college, Wilma returned to the Olympics. This time, in Rome, Italy, she won three gold medals!

Wilma Rudolph had a rough start in life. She was born two months early and weighed only 4 1/2 pounds. Then, when she was four years old she caught polio, a virus that weakens people's muscles and sometimes paralyzes them. Wilma was 12

when she finally took off the heavy metal leg braces she had needed to walk. Now she was ready for her next challenge—becoming a basketball star.

With her legs in braces, Wilma had spent years watching her brothers and sisters play the game. By the time Wilma was in high school, she was an excellent basketball player.

When Wilma was in tenth grade, a track coach noticed her fast sprints down the basketball court. He invited her to train in track and field with other high school students at Tennessee State University. Later, Coach Temple encouraged Wilma to try out for the Olympic Games to be held in Melbourne, Australia. In 1956, at 16, Wilma became

In her career, Wilma Rudolph received dozens of awards, including the 1962 Babe Didrickson Zaharias Award, which is given to the most outstanding athlete in the world. That same year, she retired from track competition. In 1981, she started the Wilma Rudolph Foundation, a group that gives free coaching to young athletes.

It's a Fact
Wilma was the 20th of 22 children in her family.

Steven Spielberg
Born December 18, 1947, in Cincinnati, Ohio
Family Married Amy Irving; one child. Married Kate Capshaw; five children
Claim to Fame Hollywood movie producer, director, and writer who has made some of the most successful movies of all time

Steven Spielberg has always enjoyed scaring people. When he was a boy, he especially loved to frighten his younger sisters. One time he scared them by wrapping his face in a mask of toilet paper and pretending to be a mummy. Another time he hid outside a sister's window and made noises to scare her.

Steven also enjoyed taking pictures and making movies. He was only 12 when he used his toy trains and a small movie camera to film "train wrecks." His parents helped him by setting up miniature movie sets around the house.

It is fitting, then, that Steven grew up to make movies, sometimes scary ones. He began his career while he was still a student at California State College—Long Beach. Trying to attract the attention of Hollywood professionals, he made a short movie, *Amblin'.* It did the trick. Shortly before his 21st birthday, Universal Studios

E.T. visits planet Earth

offered him a contract to direct shows for TV. Steven became the youngest director ever signed to a long-term Hollywood contract.

Steven Spielberg used his love of suspense and special effects in many successful action movies, including *Jaws, E.T., Raiders of the Lost Ark,* and *Jurassic Park.* He also made movies with serious themes. *The Color Purple,* based on a novel by Alice Walker, tells the story of an African-American woman. *Schindler's List* is based on a real person, Oskar Schindler, and his efforts to save hundreds of Jews from death at the hands of the German army in Poland, Germany, and Austria during World War II.

It's a Fact
Schindler's List won seven Academy Awards (Oscars), including best film and best director of 1993.

SALLY RIDE

Sally Ride
Born May 26, 1951, in Los Angeles, California
Family Married Steven A. Hawley
Claim to Fame Scientist who became the first American woman to fly in space

From the time Sally Ride was little, she loved sports. She read the sports pages, and could slug a softball better than any other kid in her neighborhood.

Sally loved science, too—especially astronomy, the study of stars and other heavenly bodies. Sally was in college when Neil Armstrong became

the first person to walk on the moon. She was thrilled about the news. But she knew she couldn't become an astronaut herself because there were no women in the U.S. space program.

In 1964, the Civil Rights Act was passed. Title IX of this act guaranteed women the same job

opportunities as men. Sally worked hard and applied to the space program, along with 8,000 other young scientists. Her outstanding math and

science background, her physical fitness, and her calm personality made her perfect for the job. In 1978, she was chosen to start astronaut training. Five years later, on June 18, 1983, she boarded the space shuttle *Challenger* as the first American woman to fly in space. She was also the youngest American astronaut ever to fly.

What did Sally have to say about orbiting 200 miles above Earth? She said, "I'm sure it was the most fun I'll ever have in my life."

It's a Fact
Sally Ride was an excellent tennis player who was ranked 28th in the country when she was in her teens. She even thought of making tennis her career.

I n every age, great people often get to meet and know other great people. Here are a few pairs who knew each other—some slightly, others well.

One of **Daniel Boone**'s best boyhood friends was Abraham Lincoln, whose grandson became **President Abraham Lincoln**. President Lincoln was proud of the association because he considered Boone a real American hero.

From 1784 to 1785, **Abigail Adams** lived with her family in Auteuil (oh-TIE), just outside Paris. **Benjamin Franklin** was also in Paris, working with Abigail's husband, John, on trade agreements with France. Franklin sometimes visited the Adamses. But Abigail was much more friendly with Thomas Jefferson, who was then Ambassador to France.

Clara Barton met **Susan B. Anthony** on November 30, 1867, in a train station in Cleveland. They became good friends. In 1906, Barton wrote this about Anthony:

A few days ago, someone said to me that every woman should stand with bared head before Susan B. Anthony. "Yes," I answered, "and every man as well."

In 1885, **Walt Whitman** was old and poor. **Mark Twain** was one of several friends and admirers who gave money to buy a horse and buggy as a surprise gift for Whitman. Whitman was delighted with his present and drove everywhere in it.

Alexander Graham Bell first met with **Helen Keller** in 1886, when Helen was six years old. Bell was very important in Helen's life; he put Helen's parents in touch with Dr. Anagnos, who suggested Anne Sullivan as a teacher for Helen. When Bell saw Helen again in 1888, they had a conversation using the manual alphabet. Helen said, "He talked very fast with his fingers about lions and tigers and elephants."

In 1909, **Andrew Carnegie** offered **Helen Keller** an annual income as a reward for her outstanding contributions as a public figure. In a very nice letter, Helen refused the money. She explained, "[I want to] fight my battles without further help than I am now receiving."

In 1935, **Irving Berlin** was in Hollywood for the filming of the musical *Top Hat*, for which he had written all the songs. **Lucille Ball** had a tiny part as a flower shop clerk. In 1936, she was in another Berlin musical, *Follow the Fleet*. This time she had more lines, as a character named Kitty Collins.

In February 1937, **Martha Graham** danced at the White House for the President and First Lady, Franklin and **Eleanor Roosevelt**. Martha was the first American dancer to perform there. On her way out to catch a midnight train, she met Eleanor in the lobby. Eleanor was ordering the next day's dinner. She stopped what she was doing to embrace Martha warmly and say, "How kind of you to come, how very kind to have made the effort to come!"

In 1963, **Martin Luther King, Jr.** was arrested for leading protests in Birmingham, Alabama. **Jackie Robinson** and King had been friendly for some time. Both men were involved in the NAACP. Jackie and his wife, Rachel, worked hard to raise the money for King's bail.

In 1981, when **Sandra Day O'Connor** joined the Supreme Court, she became a colleague of **Thurgood Marshall**. Justice Marshall served on the court from 1967 until 1991, when he retired. They often did not agree on cases, but Sandra looked up to Marshall. Shortly before he died in 1993, she wrote this about him: "He is a man who sees the world exactly as it is and pushes on to make it what it can become."

Stickers

Irving Berlin • Page 35

Martha Graham • Page 36

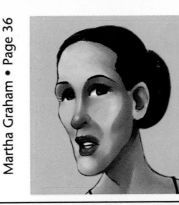

Babe Ruth • Page 37

Amelia Earhart • Page 38

Walt Disney • Page 40

Margaret Mead • Page 41

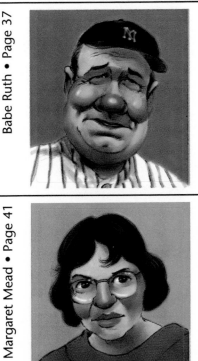

Langston Hughes • Page 42

Marian Anderson • Page 43

Thurgood Marshall • Page 44

Lucille Ball • Page 45

Rosa Parks • Page 46

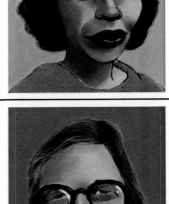

Jesse Owens • Page 47

Jonas Salk • Page 48

I. M. Pei • Page 49

50 Great Americans
Every Kid Should Know
Stickers

Abigail Van Buren, Ann Landers • Page 50

Jackie Robinson • Page 52

Cesar Chavez • Page 53

Maya Angelou • Page 54

James Watson • Page 55

Martin Luther King, Jr. • Page 56

Sandra Day O'Connor • Page 57

Neil Armstrong • Page 58

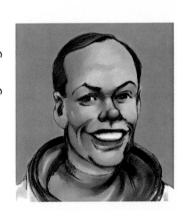

Wilma Rudolph • Page 59

Steven Spielberg • Page 60

Sally Ride • Page 61